ARE THEY REAL?

WITCHES

by Tristan Poehlmann

BrightPoint Press

San Diego, CA

BrightPoint Press

an imprint of ReferencePoint Press, Inc.
Printed in the United States

For more information, contact:
BrightPoint Press
PO Box 27779
San Diego, CA 92198
www.BrightPointPress.com

LIBRARY OF CONGRESS CATALOGING-IN-PUBLICATION DATA

Names: Poehlmann, Tristan, author.
Title: Witches / by Tristan Poehlmann.
Description: San Diego, CA: BrightPoint Press, [2024] | Series: Are they real? | Includes bibliographical references and index. | Audience: Ages 13 | Audience: Grades 7-9
Identifiers: LCCN 2023004120 (print) | LCCN 2023004121 (eBook) | ISBN 9781678206383 (hardcover) | ISBN 9781678206390 (eBook)
Subjects: LCSH: Witches--History--Juvenile literature. | Witchcraft--History--Juvenile literature.
Classification: LCC BF1566 .P63 2024 (print) | LCC BF1566 (eBook) | DDC 133.4/3--dc23/eng/20230415
LC record available at https://lccn.loc.gov/2023004120
LC eBook record available at https://lccn.loc.gov/2023004121

CONTENTS

AT A GLANCE 4

INTRODUCTION 6
THE INJURED WITCH

CHAPTER ONE 12
WHAT IS A WITCH?

CHAPTER TWO 24
THE HISTORY OF WITCHES

CHAPTER THREE 36
LOOKING AT THE EVIDENCE

CHAPTER FOUR 48
THE CULTURAL IMPACT OF WITCHES

Glossary 58
Source Notes 59
For Further Research 60
Index 62
Image Credits 63
About the Author 64

AT A GLANCE

- Witches are people who practice magic. Their magic can be either good or bad.
- The classic witch wears all black, has a big pointy hat, and flies on a broomstick.
- Witches look like humans, but people fear them because they can do magic.
- Witches are believed to do a variety of magic. This includes shape-shifting into animals, cursing people, healing, or predicting the future.
- Fear of witches is based in European folklore and history. It has led to witch hunts that killed thousands of people.
- Most witch hunts and witch trials happened between 1400 and 1800 CE. They were tied to Catholic and Protestant religious beliefs.

- In 1692, famous witch trials known as the Salem Witch Trials took place in Salem, Massachusetts.
- Many people believed that witches got their magic from working with the devil.
- Witchcraft accusations were often related to social prejudice. Women and Jewish people were the most common targets of witch accusations.
- Today, witch themes are still influential throughout North American popular culture.

INTRODUCTION

THE INJURED WITCH

A boy stepped into a forest clearing. He was tired and hungry. Ahead on a riverbank stood a run-down mill. The old mill wheel groaned as it turned. A man standing near the mill called out, “You there! Come help me! My wife will feed you supper!”

The boy knew of danger in the forest. Tales warned of witches and tricksters. But he was hungry. He decided to help the miller. All day he hauled grain. When suppertime came, the miller's wife gave him hot stew.

In some stories, witches lure people into cabins in the woods.

"I haven't had help for a week," the miller told the boy. "Our servant ran off in the night."

His wife cast him a warning look. "You may sleep in the loft," she offered the boy.

That night, the boy woke to scratching sounds. Beside his bed, glowing yellow eyes looked right at him. The boy shook with fear. He grabbed his pocketknife. "What are you?" he whispered.

A hiss filled the air. The boy's hair stood on end. He struck out with his knife. There was an angry shriek, then silence. The boy did not sleep after that. At sunrise he

Black cats are often associated with witches. Some witches are believed to be able to turn into different animals, including cats.

searched the loft. In a dark corner he found a cat's bloodied paw print. Had the night beast been only a cat?

Downstairs, the miller sat eating bread and butter. "My wife is not well enough to

Broomsticks are a witch's preferred mode of transportation. Witches use broomsticks to fly across the night sky.

cook," he explained. "It is her hand. She has bandaged it up. It was injured in the night."

The boy's heart started racing. What if the night beast had actually been a witch? He quickly left the old mill.

ARE WITCHES REAL?

People told this story across Europe. The details varied, but the basic story was the same. The tale was a warning. It warned that strange animals might be witches. It warned that witches could change form. The tale also warned that witches wanted to cause harm. But do witches really exist?

1

WHAT IS A WITCH?

Witches have been pictured in many ways throughout history. In North America, the classic witch image is often connected to Halloween. These witches wear pointy black hats with a wide brim. They wear long black gowns. Their boots are narrow and pointy. They might also wear black capes.

Witches often have black cats. They usually carry a broomstick. Witches ride their broomsticks through the night sky.

Evil witches are sometimes pictured with green skin. It marks them as being different from regular humans.

Witches use cauldrons to brew potions and poisons.

They also have cauldrons for making potions. These large pots hang over fires. They bubble full of creepy ingredients.

The word *witch* can mean many things. Typically, witches are thought of as humans who do evil magic. They are considered dangerous to their communities. But other understandings of witches are more complex. Different cultures have different beliefs about witches. For example, not all witches are believed to use magic the same way. They do not all behave the same way either.

A HUMAN CREATURE

Witches are usually shown as old women. They can look very ugly. Their faces might be bumpy and warty. Their skin might be sickly green. But sometimes witches are shown as young women. Young witches have the opposite look. They are typically very attractive. They use their looks to get people to come closer to them. Both kinds of witches can be dangerous.

WITCHY ANIMALS

Witches are believed to have a close relationship with animals such as black cats. There are several reasons for this connection. In some stories, witches can shape-shift into different creatures. Witches also sometimes have assistants called familiars. These are animals with magical traits. They will obey the witch's commands.

The image of the Halloween witch came from European **folklore**. Pointy hats and boots were traditional fashions. Black clothing sometimes represents death or evil. The witch's outfit marks her as creepy and strange. She looks like a human. But she is suspicious because she does not try to fit in.

Malcolm Gaskill is an expert on the history of witches. He teaches at the University of East Anglia in England. He explains, "Witches are *human*. Unlike monsters, they belong to society—a disguised enemy within. They are 'other,' and yet they are also ‘us.’”[1] The witch comes from humans’ fear of other humans. Witches are scary because they look human, but they can do magic. They are not obvious beasts or monsters. Any person could be a witch.

A HUMAN BELIEF

Witches often show a culture’s fears and beliefs. Different belief systems can create different witchlike figures. All witches use a magical or spiritual power. But how they use that power can be considered either good or bad. Witches can use their power in

A group or gathering of witches is known as a coven.

many ways. Some are healers. Others can predict the future. But some witches are thought to use their powers to harm people.

Throughout history, witches have been seen as evil beings. They are often **accused** of doing evil acts. Witches are said to **curse** people, animals, and crops. Accusations of hurting babies and children

WHERE DO WITCHES COME FROM?

The word *witch* comes from Old English. It was originally *wicca* or *wicce*. The words were pronounced "witchah" and "witchuh." They meant a man or woman who did magic. Wicca and wicce practiced witchcraft, or wiccecraeft. *Craft* or *craeft* meant a learned skill.

are especially common. Witches are also believed to cause injuries, deaths, or natural disasters. Many people of the Christian faith consider the representation of witchcraft and those who practice it to be sinful.

However, there are other people who believe in good witches and positive magic. There are some people in modern culture who identify as witches. They often practice religions like Wicca. Most of these kinds of witches aim to use magic as a force for good. But many people today still closely link witches with wickedness.

Throughout history, many people believed witches could do rituals that would summon the devil.

Groups of witches are sometimes seen as devil-worshipping **cults**. This belief comes from European religious traditions. Norman Cohn taught history at the University of Sussex. He writes that witches were often said to worship the devil. Cohn explains that people thought witches “adhered to a religious cult that was not only non-Christian but anti-Christian.”[2]

Cohn found no historical proof for this claim. Devil-worshipping witch cults did not exist. However, this religious connection to witches remains culturally important in North America. Today, some people still believe those who practice witchcraft are evil. And sometimes witches continue to be portrayed as devil worshippers in pop culture.

2

THE HISTORY OF WITCHES

The idea of magic is ancient. Most early societies believed in magic. Early humans thought magic controlled natural events. Much later, European Christians believed magic was an evil idea. Many European countries invaded other societies. They would punish societies they thought used magic. The European view of magic had a global impact. Today, using magic is often called witchcraft. Some societies view witches as evil. Others have complex or mixed beliefs.

Witches are typically seen as ugly old women who want to harm people, especially children.

Some witches write down potions or spells in books.

Magic has been a useful way for humans to explain terrible events. Elaine G. Breslaw studies the history of witchcraft. She used to teach at the University of Tennessee. Breslaw says humans have used witchcraft to "explain the presence of evil, to establish a cause for misfortune and disease, to justify natural occurrences like storms and earthquakes, to give meaning to mysterious events, to provide answers to problems that seemingly defied reasonable explanations."[3] People believed that witchcraft held power. They feared magic. So, they created ways to identify and punish witches.

WITCH HUNTS

Historically, the purpose of witch hunts was to accuse people who were believed to be doing witchcraft. Witch hunts often began with someone having a complaint about someone else. Even if the complaint was made up, a community might still believe it. Gaskill explains, "Peak periods of witch-hunting correspond with war, plague, and harvest failure."[4] Events like these triggered fear. Communities feared

WITCHES AND CHILDREN

Many stories claim that witches want to steal children. The story "Hansel and Gretel" is one example of that claim. In the story, a witch plans to bake children into a pie. Other tales claim witches steal children's blood. Claims like this were linked to **anti-Semitism**. Jewish people were often accused of witchcraft and stealing children.

violence, sickness, and starvation. They wanted to blame a **scapegoat** for their bad luck. Witch hunts gave people an enemy to blame. They also distracted communities from larger problems. The people accused of witchcraft became the focus. Witches had to be punished. Many people accused of witchcraft were assaulted, driven away, or killed.

Witches have been scapegoats throughout history. European fears were built into the witch's image. This is clear from her characteristics. Witches were often seen as evil old women. They were women

In pop culture, witches are often pictured wearing black because it is associated with evil or death.

with too much power. Witches were also linked to false views about Jewish people. Christians branded both groups as devil worshippers. Parts of witch folklore are based in anti-Semitic beliefs.

In the 1500s CE, a wave of witch hunts swept across Europe. It was a result of the Protestant Reformation. This was a religious movement that created a new branch of Christianity. It was called Protestantism. The new Protestant churches gave power to local authorities. People passed local laws based on religion. Witches became more than a religious enemy. They became a legal enemy as well.

WITCH TRIALS

The increased local control due to the Protestant Reformation meant communities had the power to pass legal judgment. Breslaw explains, "Local authorities, particularly in Scotland and Puritan New England, sometimes caught up in panics about supposed witchcraft, took matters into their own hands."[5] Witch hunts became witch trials. And local judgment was often **biased**.

Local authorities would often torture people accused of witchcraft. This was sometimes legal. But even where it was illegal, it was still common. Many people believed torture revealed the truth. The goal of torture was to produce a confession.

People who were accused of being witches were often considered guilty by the community before they even went to trial.

The accused who would not confess to doing witchcraft were treated worse. And forced confessions could be used in court.

In 1692, famous witch trials began in North America. They were known as the Salem Witch Trials. In Europe, witch trials were becoming less common. But Salem, Massachusetts, had an outbreak of accusations. Rumors of witchcraft grew into a community panic. Between 150 and 200 people were accused. Around twenty people were executed. Another five died in jail. Witchcraft accusations tore the community apart. The Salem Witch Trials are remembered as a warning against **persecution**.

Tens of thousands of people were killed as witches during the height of witch hunts. Many who survived lost family, homes, and social standing. And historians have concluded that many of the accused probably did not even practice witchcraft.

SALEM WITCH TRIALS EXECUTIONS, 1692

June 10 — The execution of Bridget Bishop is the first recorded execution.

July 19 — Rebecca Nurse, Susannah Martin, Elizabeth Howe, Sarah Good, and Sarah Wildes are executed.

August 19 — George Jacobs, Martha Carrier, George Burroughs, John Proctor, and John Willard are hanged.

September 19 — Giles Corey is pressed to death under heavy stones.

September 22 — The executions of Martha Corey, Margaret Scott, Mary Easty, Alice Parker, Ann Pudeator, Wilmot Redd, Samuel Wardwell, and Mary Parker are the last recorded executions.

Source: "Salem Witch Trials Chronology," Salem Witch Museum, *n.d. https://salemwitchmuseum.com*

Around twenty people were executed during the Salem Witch Trials between June and September of 1692.

3

LOOKING AT THE EVIDENCE

Before 1400 CE, European witch hunts were rare. But around that time, a new witch figure emerged. This created the idea of the modern witch that is often represented in pop culture today. The image came from early European folklore. Tales described night flying women who did dark or evil magic. Witchlike figures were said to steal and eat children.

These beliefs about witches are myths, not true stories. Professor Robert W. Thurston studies witch history. He used to teach at Miami University. Thurston writes

The Salem Witch Museum is located in Salem, Massachusetts. It features the history of both the European and Salem witch trials.

that the panic about witch cults comes from human fear. He explains, "The European imagination could create such creatures—for there is no credible evidence that they really existed."[6]

DID WITCHES REALLY EXIST?

Early witch stories were unrelated to Christianity. But church leaders knew of them. Some images of witches in folklore seemed similar to Christian imagery. Church leaders began to use the folklore images in their own religious imagery. They added witch figures into scenes of devil worship.

Throughout history, pentacles have often been seen as a symbol for the devil. But to practicing witches, pentacles symbolize protection.

For Christians, the witch figure became a devil worshipper.

Ronald Hutton is a historian at the University of Bristol. He explains that in the 1400s, witches were considered bad because their beliefs opposed Christian beliefs. Hutton also says the church believed the devil gave witches powers to harm people. This belief often made local people panic. The church used its writings to help grow the idea that witches worked with the devil.

The Christian image of the witch spread. The belief led to witch hunts. After the Protestant Reformation in the 1500s, witch

EYE OF NEWT

Ingredients that are often associated with witches' potions have interesting names. One ingredient is called eye of newt. But names can deceive. These ingredients come from plants. Eye of newt is a mustard seed. Toe of frog is a buttercup. Tongue of dog is another flower. Old ingredient names described what a plant part looked like.

hunts increased. The people who were targeted were often women.

FEMALE WITCHES

The first witch hunts did not always focus on women. Some men were accused of being witches too. However, women became the focus of witch hunts in the 1400s. Church leaders wrote witch hunting guides to help people identify witches. Many women were suddenly in danger of being seen as witches.

Women were accused of witchcraft for many reasons. During this time period,

Most witch hunts around the world occurred between the 1400s and 1800s.

women were seen as mothers, wives, or caretakers. They were sometimes accused of being a witch if others believed they were not behaving as they should. Other times, women were thought to be witches if they held too much power. These were women who were seen as having more authority in the community than the men did.

Witch hunts reflected a common belief about women. Breslaw explains, “Women were suspected in deaths of infants and all kinds of misdeeds in the care of children and the preparation of food. But they could also come under suspicion for causing storms and other natural disasters.”[7] About 75 percent of those killed during witch hunts were women.

WHAT REALLY HAPPENED?

The Salem Witch Trials began with a few accusations. But more accusations continued to happen. Historians have tried to understand why. One explanation might be a community-wide panic. Some experts have suggested that poison could be one possible explanation. Rye grain can grow fungus that causes hallucinations. A fungus may have poisoned Salem's rye crops.

The most likely explanation for the accusations is extreme stress. The colony of Massachusetts was in political and social crisis during that time. People in

Flowers and herbs are common ingredients used in witch potions.

Salem felt afraid and threatened. Witchcraft offered them a scapegoat. In a panic, they persecuted innocent people. Pointless suffering destroyed people's lives.

In Europe and North America, witch trials were unjust. People were often questioned under torture. This forced many people to confess. In some places, confession could

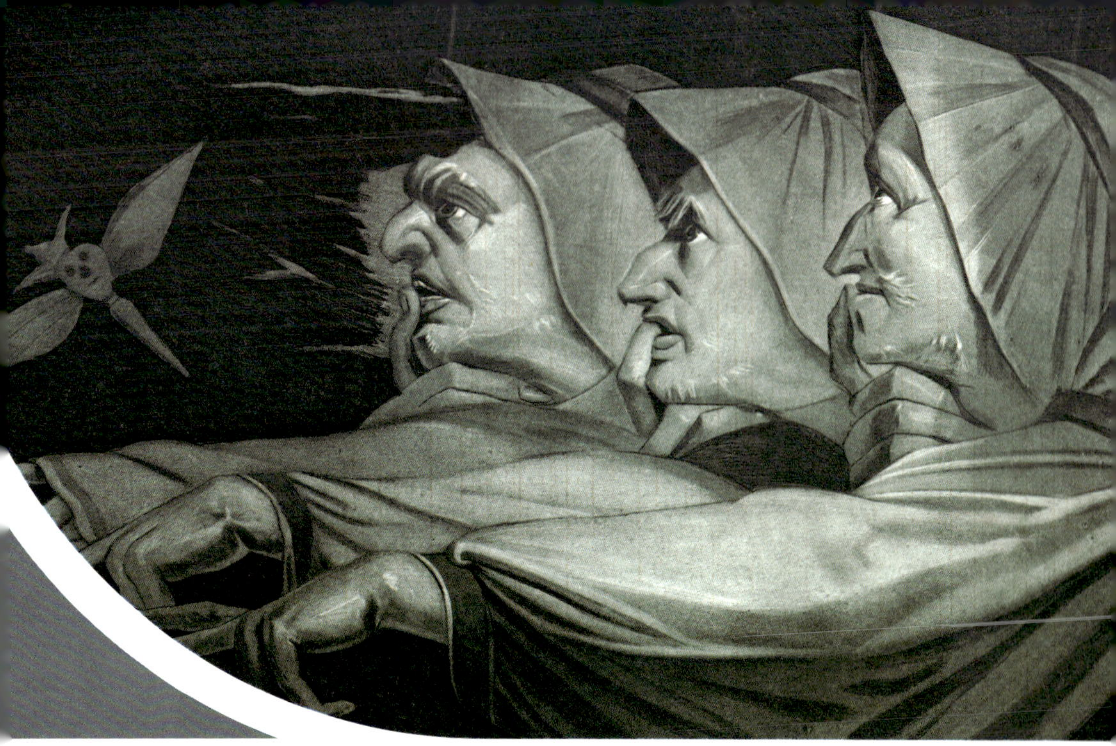

William Shakespeare's play Macbeth features three witches known as the Weird or Wayward Sisters.

save people from death. Accusing others could also save people's lives. People would tell lies to stop the fear and pain.

RECORDING WITCH HISTORY

By 1800 CE, witch hunts had nearly disappeared. Experts say around 40,000 to 60,000 people were killed between the 1400s and 1800s. Some believe it might have been more than that. Not all records survived. Many witch hunts and legal witch trials were officially documented. But many were not. Gaskill explains, "Legal documents that have revealed so much are silent about the millions of suspicions, accusations, assaults, and lynchings that never reached the courts."[8] It may never be known how many people were actually killed as a result of witch hunts.

4
THE CULTURAL IMPACT OF WITCHES

Witches are everywhere in North America. Their image is deep in US culture. From religion to movies, witches have had a huge cultural impact. They show up in holidays like Halloween and in fears. The modern witch image still holds complex meanings.

WITCHES IN REALITY

Some people call themselves witches in real life. This includes people who practice the Wiccan religion. It developed during the mid-1900s. *Wicca* is the Old English word for witch. Wiccan practices focus

Dressing up as a witch is a popular Halloween costume in the United States.

on ancient, nature-centered magic. For example, Wiccans celebrate the seasonal changes. They consider themselves witches in the pre-Christian tradition. Those who practice the Wiccan religion are not interested in the devil. Their moral code is to harm none and use their magic for good.

TOIL AND TROUBLE

Double, double toil and trouble;
Fire burn and cauldron bubble.

Many people know this chant. It often makes people think of witches. Fewer people know where it comes from. William Shakespeare wrote it. His play *Macbeth* begins with three witches called the Weird Sisters. They cast a spell to see the future.

WITCHES IN ENTERTAINMENT

Witches are often featured in fantasy stories. The 1937 movie *Snow White and the Seven Dwarfs* featured the Evil Queen. She was an elegant, cruel witch. In 1939, Hollywood created classic American witches. *The Wizard of Oz* used new color film technology. The Wicked Witch of the West was literally green with envy. Glinda, the Good Witch of the North, looked like a glittery princess. Those images became popular in witch culture.

Witch folklore changed in the 2000s. The Harry Potter series of books and movies imagined an alternate magical world. Hermione Granger was a talented good witch. There were also bad witches like Bellatrix Lestrange. The Harry Potter series is an example of modern witch fantasy. Stories about being a witch have become very popular.

Other stories still include evil witches. Horror films that use witches can be very scary. *The Blair Witch Project* told a witchy urban legend. The 1999 film was made to look like footage from a personal video camera. It made people think the events really happened. In 2016, *The Witch* was

Witches and wizards use wands to cast spells in the Harry Potter series. Hermione Granger is known to be one of the best witches.

released. This movie was set in New England around the late 1600s. The film used both a modern fear of witches and the history of witch hunts to scare its viewers.

WITCH CONSPIRACY THEORIES

Stories about witches tend to reveal cultural fears. Experts connect modern fears to older ones. Witches were accused of poisoning children's food. Today, people still fear that others want to harm children. Gaskill explains, "In the early 1980s, a survey found that 70% of Americans believed in the existence of . . . cults preying on children."[9]

In the 1980s, the **conspiracy theory** about devil worshipping cults grew. Another kind of witch hunt began. It was known as the Satanic Panic. The Satanic Panic was

Modern portrayals of witches sometimes include magic that comes from nature and is used to do good.

a series of false accusations against day care centers. People believed the workers were abusing kids by using them in satanic rituals. Much like old witch hunts, the Satanic Panic ruined many people's lives.

Witches remain an important part of modern culture and entertainment today.

Fear of witchlike cults was an obvious element of these accusations.

Similar conspiracy theories continue to return in modern culture. Today, they exist and spread online. These stories about witches rely on very old rumors. But they also rely on ignorance of history. Historians say there is no evidence evil witches ever existed as an organized group.

Today, witches exist in folklore, religion, and modern culture. They also exist in people who identify as witches and practice the Wiccan religion. But people are still drawn to scary witch stories. They reflect human fears, just as they have for hundreds of years.

GLOSSARY

accused

charged with a fault or crime

anti-Semitism

prejudice or hatred against Jewish people

biased

being for or against someone or something in an unfair way

conspiracy theory

a belief that a secret organization is responsible for an event or phenomenon

cults

unusual or secretive systems of religious worship

curse

to use magic or other powers to cause harm to someone or something

folklore

traditional customs, beliefs, stories, and sayings

persecution

cruel or harmful treatment of a particular group of people

scapegoat

a person who is forced to take the blame for others

SOURCE NOTES

CHAPTER ONE: WHAT IS A WITCH?

1. Malcolm Gaskill, *Witchcraft: A Very Short Introduction*. New York: Oxford University Press, 2010, p. 1. https://archive.org.

2. Quoted in Elaine G. Breslaw, ed., *Witches of the Atlantic World: An Historical Reader and Primary Sourcebook*. New York: New York University Press, 2000, p. 52. https://archive.org.

CHAPTER TWO: THE HISTORY OF WITCHES

3. Breslaw, *Witches of the Atlantic World: An Historical Reader and Primary Sourcebook*, p. 3.

4. Gaskill, *Witchcraft: A Very Short Introduction*, p. 71.

5. Breslaw, *Witches of the Atlantic World: An Historical Reader and Primary Sourcebook*, p. 8.

CHAPTER THREE: LOOKING AT THE EVIDENCE

6. Robert Thurston, *The Witch Hunts: A History of the Witch Persecutions in Europe and North America*. New York: Routledge, 2006, p. 8.

7. Breslaw, *Witches of the Atlantic World: An Historical Reader and Primary Sourcebook*, p. 283.

8. Gaskill, *Witchcraft: A Very Short Introduction*, p. 71.

CHAPTER FOUR: THE CULTURAL IMPACT OF WITCHES

9. Gaskill, *Witchcraft: A Very Short Introduction*, p. 26.

FOR FURTHER RESEARCH

BOOKS

Virginia Loh-Hagan, *Salem Witch Trials.* Ann Arbor, MI: 45th Parallel Press, 2020.

Carla Mooney, *ESP.* San Diego, CA: BrightPoint Press, 2023.

Matt Ralphs, *Season of the Witch: A Spellbinding History of Witches and Other Magical Folk.* New York: Flying Eye Books, 2020.

INTERNET SOURCES

"Halloween," *DK Find Out!*, n.d. www.dkfindout.com.

"The Salem Witch Trials of 1692," *Peabody Essex Museum*, n.d. https://my.matterport.com.

"Witches and Magic," *Shakespeare's Globe*, n.d. www.shakespearesglobe.com.

WEBSITES

Interactive Witch Trial

www.historicnorthampton.org/interactive-witch-trial

The Historic Northampton Museum has an interactive witch trial game called "Is Mary Bliss Parsons a Witch?" The game helps to educate people on what it would have been like to live through the trial of Mary Bliss Parsons, a real person who was accused of doing witchcraft in the 1600s.

Salem Witch Museum

https://salemwitchmuseum.com

The Salem Witch Museum features information about the Salem Witch Trials. The site shares history of the trials and has an online tour of notable locations where the witch trials occurred.

Witches: The Myth and Magic

https://westportlibrary.libguides.com/witches

The Westport Library shares information on the history of and myths about witches and witchcraft. The site includes videos, books, and articles for people to further their learning about witches.

INDEX

black, 9, 12–13, 16, 17, 30
Blair Witch Project, The, 52
broomsticks, 10, 13

cats, 9, 13, 16
cauldrons, 14, 50
children, 20, 25, 28, 37, 43, 54
Christianity, 21, 23, 24, 30–31, 38–40, 50
confessions, 32–33, 45
conspiracy theories, 54, 56
cults, 22–23, 38, 54, 56
curses, 20

devil worship, 22–23, 30, 38–40, 50, 54

Europe, 11, 17, 22, 24–25, 29, 31, 33, 36, 37, 38, 45
evil, 13, 15, 17, 20, 23, 24–25, 27, 29, 30, 37, 51–52, 57
executions, 34, 35

green skin, 13, 16, 51

Halloween, 12, 17, 48, 49
Harry Potter, 51–52, 53
hats, 12, 17

ingredients, 14, 40, 45

Judaism, 28, 30

Macbeth, 46, 50
magic, 15, 16, 18, 20, 21, 24–27, 37, 50, 52, 55

North America, 12, 23, 33, 45, 48, 51, 54

potions, 14, 26, 40, 45
Protestant Reformation, 31, 40

religion, 21–23, 31, 38, 48, 49–50, 57
rituals, 22, 55

Salem Witch Trials, 33–34, 35, 37, 44–45
Satanic Panic, 54–55
scapegoats, 29, 45
Snow White and the Seven Dwarfs, 51

torture, 32, 45

Wicca, 20, 21, 49–50, 57
Witch, The, 52
witch hunts, 27–29, 31, 32, 34, 36, 40–41, 42, 43, 46–47, 53, 54–55
Wizard of Oz, The, 51
women witches, 15–16, 20, 25, 29, 36, 41–43

IMAGE CREDITS

ABOUT THE AUTHOR

Tristan Poehlmann is a freelance writer of educational nonfiction. A museum exhibit developer for many years, he also holds a master's degree in writing for children and young adults from Vermont College of Fine Arts. He lives in the San Francisco Bay Area.